Aloha,

My name is Lahela Chandler Correa. I was born and raised on the beautiful island of Kaua'i in the Wainiha Valley.   Two miles from where I lived, my 'ohana farmed a 5 acre kalo (taro) field which provided food for ourselves and the community.

My parents Francis Sr. and Kapeka Chandler were born and raised in Hā'ena.   They both came from a large 'ohana (family).   In my immediate family I have 10 brothers, 5 sisters and one half sister. I am number 13 of all my siblings.

Both my parents were great examples of Aloha. They showed us "Aloha" by living it every day. They taught us that Aloha was taking care of your family, being kind to everyone, being helpful, being honest, always setting a good example, working hard, doing your best, keeping our name good and always respecting your elders.

For me "Aloha" is not just a word, it has a deeper meaning that is endless. Like all things in life if not passed down and taught, it will be forgotten.

Aloha is a way of life that was taught for generations to our people. This is who we are, we live it, we breath it every day of our lives. This is how the first foreigners were greeted when they came here. Aloha means that when we meet someone they are greeted with utmost kindness. When we offer to do something, nothing is expected in return and when we share we give freely.

It doesn't matter if you are white, black, blue or green, I believe we all have "Aloha". Aloha is considered the gift of the Hawaiian people to the world. Learn and share Aloha today.

Aloha,
Lahela

Lahela's lineage stretches across and touches many islands.

    Her father Francis's genealogy comes from Maui and Kaua'i. His ancestors, the Kanialamas, were the genealogists and attendants to Queen Emma and her family. The families were one of the early migrators from Tahiti and whose offspring eventually settled on Kaua'i and set roots in Kahili near Kīlauea, Kaua'i.

    Her Mother Elizabeth comes from the Mahuiki and 'Īlālā'ole lines from Hā'ena, Kaua'i and Puna on Hawai'i Island respectively. The Mahuiki Family is famous for their knowledge of fishing in the Hā'ena area.

    The 'Īlālā'oles are from Puna and are descendants of Kamehameha I.

1

This book belongs to:_____

My Hawaiian name is:_____

Hawai'i is a very special place that is strong in its culture, traditions and language.

The core of the Hawaiian culture is 'ohana.

Aloha – "What it Means to my 'Ohana and Yours" supports these values.

On the Cover - MAKANA MOUNTAIN

Makana is located on northern shore of Kauaʻi, where it rises 1,115 feet above Limahuli Valley and is the beginning of the NaPali Coast. It is known by some as Bali Hai as filmed in the movie South Pacific. Makana means gift in the Hawaiian language. Lahela was born and raised under the watchful presence of this magnificent mountain.

Hawaiian Language - Did you know??

*The Hawaiian language (ʻŌlelo Hawaiʻi) is one of the oldest living languages in the world.

*When Hawaiʻi was annexed as a territory of the U.S. in 1891, the language was officially banned from the Government and schools, even at Kamehameha a private school for children of Hawaiian descent. The people were still allowed to speak Hawaiian and printed newspapers in their native language.

*Finally, in 1978, the Hawaiian language was recognized as one of the official languages, along with English in the state of Hawaiʻi.

The Hawaiian alphabet

There are 5 vowels A, E, I , O , U and 8 consonants H, K, L, M, N, P & W (V)
An ʻ okina creates a pause like in "uh - oh".   A kahakō (line over the o) creates an elongated vowel sound.

A = "ah" like in a lot	ā
E = "ey" or "ay" like in whey	ē
I = "ee" like in marine	ī
O = "o" like in older	ō
U = "oo" like in spoon	ū

Useful words/phrases to know and understand

A hui hou – until we meet again
Beach – kahakai
Breadfruit tree – ʻulu
Canoe - waʻa
Coconut - niu (nee-oo)
Child - keiki (kay-kee)
Elder - kupuna
Family - ʻohana
Fish - iʻa
Flower - pua
Friend – hoaloha
Hana hou - one more time
Help - kōkua
Kalo – taro
Land- ʻāina

Kane – man, male
Luau – Hawaiian Feast
Mauka –towards the mountain or mountain side
Makai – towards the ocean or ocean side
Nice - ʻoluʻolu
Ono – type of fish or delicious
Ocean - moana
Pau hana – done working
Pineapple – hala kahiki
Poi – Thick paste to eat made from kalo (taro)
Rainbow - ānuenue (ah-noo-weh-noo-weh)
Thank You – Mahalo (mah-hah-loh)
Thank You Very Much - Mahalo nui
Visitor – malihini
Wahine – lady, female

Words of Wisdom -   **Kuʻia kahele aka naʻau haʻahaʻa** – *(A Humble Person Walks Carefully So As Not To Hurt Others.)*

HAWAIIAN ISLANDS

Did you know? The state fish of Hawai'i is Humuhumunukunukuāpua'a

_____

_____

_____

_____

_____

P_____ Ocean

_____

Label and color the Islands above

Hawai'i Island - **'Ula'ula (red)**   **O'ahu -** **Melemele (yellow)**

Kaua'i - **Poni (purple)**   **Maui -** **'Akala (pink)**

Ni'ihau – **Polū (light blue)**   **Lāna'i -** **'Alani (orange)**

Kaho'olawe - **'Āhinahina (gray)**   **Moloka'i -** **'Ōma'oma'o (green)**

Did you know?? On May 1 in Hawai'i, we celebrate May Day which is Lei Day. The celebration consists of many festivities. There is a royal court procession, part of which are eight princesses that represent each island, dressed in their island's color and lei. The lei's are made from each islands chosen flower or shell. Many schools celebrate with hula and other cultural events.

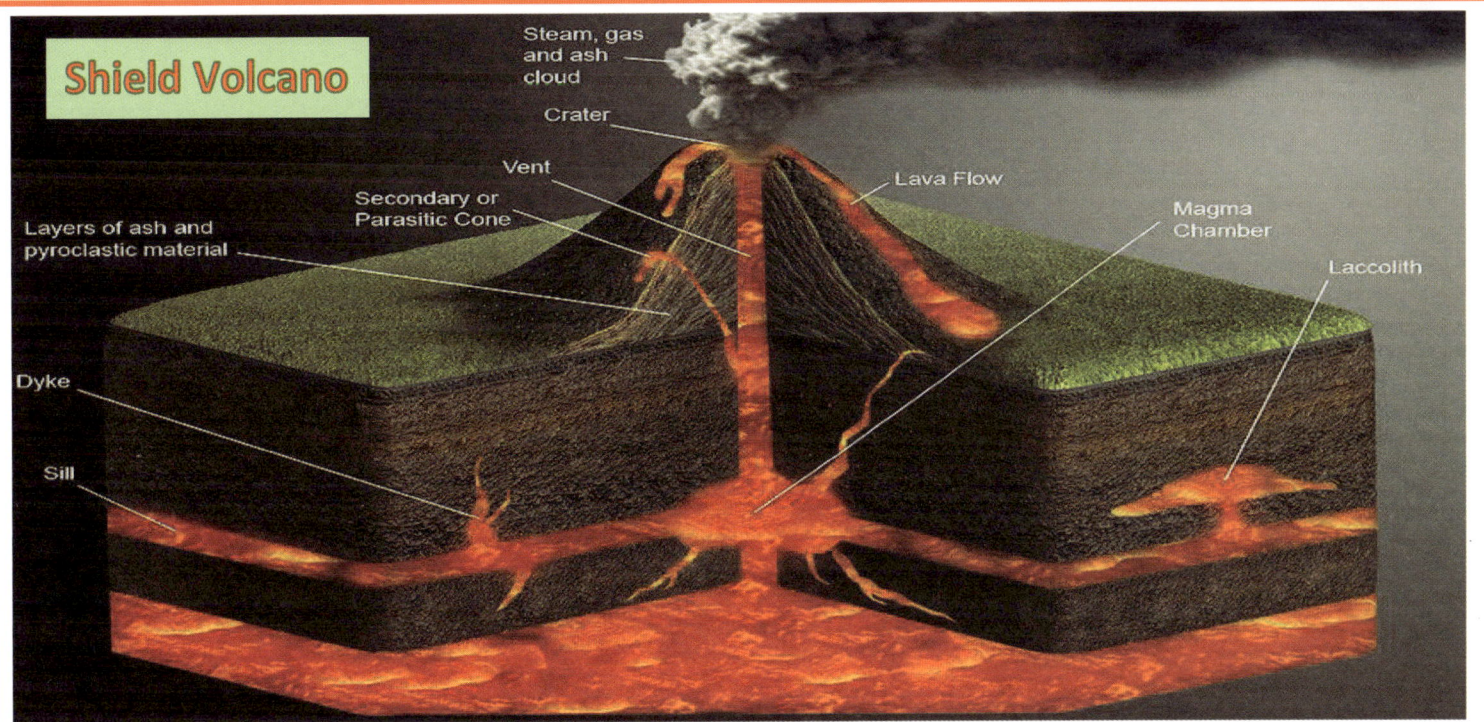

Shield Volcano

Steam, gas and ash cloud
Crater
Vent
Secondary or Parasitic Cone
Lava Flow
Magma Chamber
Laccolith
Layers of ash and pyroclastic material
Dyke
Sill

There are different types of volcanoes in the world, but the Hawaiian Islands are formed by shield volcanoes. The earth is made up of giant slabs and as they move on the ocean floor, they travel over areas called hotspots which turns the rocks into a liquid substance called magma. As seen in the picture it rises through the vent and erupts and shoots out lava. As lava cools it turns into volcanic rock which is how the islands were formed. The island of Hawai'i, is now on top of the hotspot that Kaua'i was on 4.5 million years ago, making it the oldest island. O'ahu was formed about 3 million years ago, then Moloka'i about 1.8 million years ago and Maui the youngest, at a little less than a million years old.

Did you know??   Interesting facts about Shield Volcanoes:
#1. When seen from above it looks like a warrior's shield; wide, but not tall like other volcanoes.
#2. Lava from shield volcanoes is more liquid and can flow further and faster creating the shield shape. #3 Maunakea is a shield volcano that is 4000 ft taller than Mount Everest, from base to peak.
There are currently 5 active volcanos in Hawai'i. On Hawai'i Island there are Mauna Loa, Kīlauea the most recent in 2018, Hualālai and, one still under water and growing is Lō'ihi. Haleakalā on Maui is still considered an active volcano.

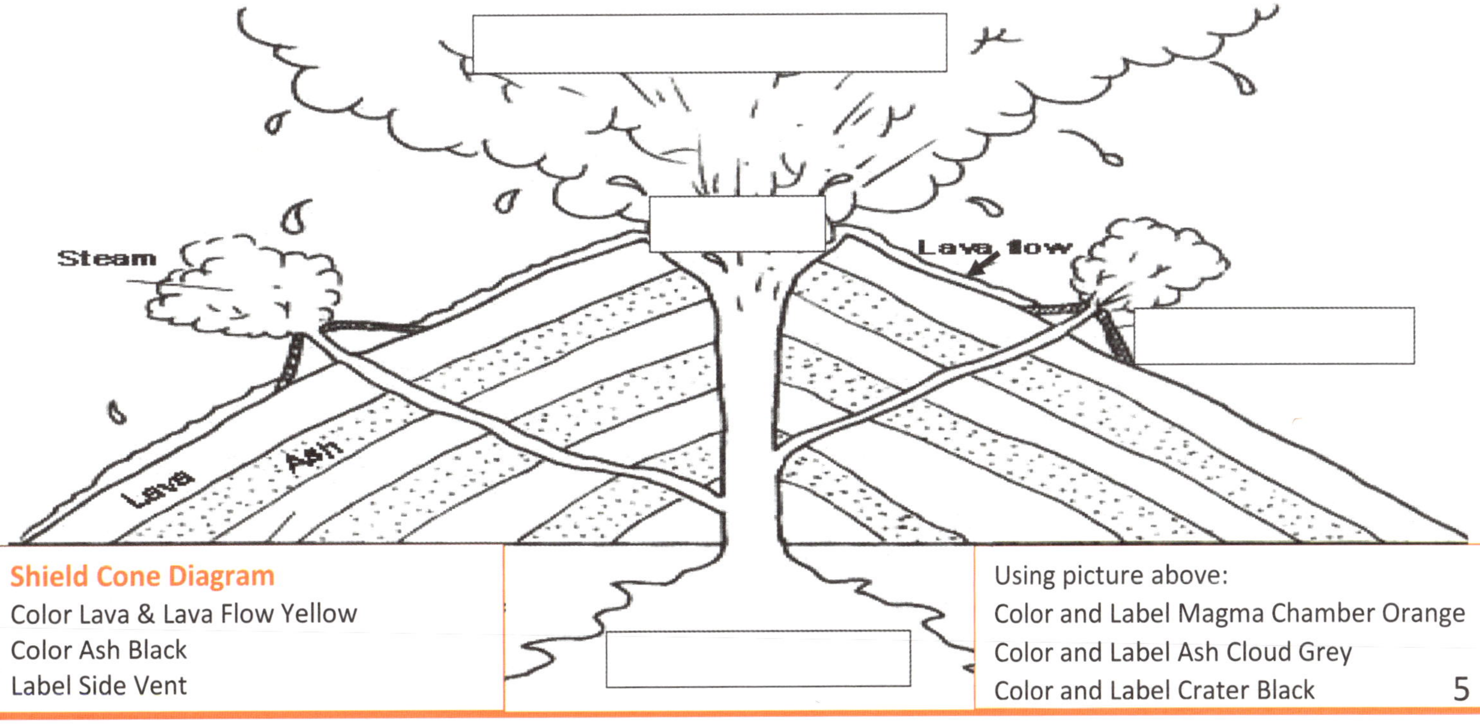

Steam

Lava flow

Lava   Ash

Shield Cone Diagram
Color Lava & Lava Flow Yellow
Color Ash Black
Label Side Vent

Using picture above:
Color and Label Magma Chamber Orange
Color and Label Ash Cloud Grey
Color and Label Crater Black

5

 # ALOHA is Akua

This means spirituality, inner peace. Like saying a **pule** (prayer; message of good wishes) before paddling a **wa'a** (outrigger canoe) in a race. This is a tradition in the **Hawaiian culture**. The **pule** can be **elua** (two) people or **elua** hundred people all closing their **nā maka** (eyes) and holding **nā lima** (hands) as the head **kupuna** (elder) shares her/his **maika'i** (good) wishes and safety for all the **kanaka hoe wa'a** (paddlers). **He aha kou mana'o?** (What do you think?)

Relax, close your eyes, take a deep breath and write what you feel. _____

_____

_____

At right, the paddlers pule before the canoe race.

 Draw a picture of a place or a person that makes you feel safe or peaceful:

'Ohana Time: Create a pule at home with your 'ohana.

Approximately 2000 years ago, **wa'a kaulua** (voyaging canoes) brought the first Polynesians to the Hawaiian Islands and have remained an important part of the history and culture.

They traveled thousands of miles over the Pacific Ocean through stormy seas and howling winds. Their **wa'a** were large and could hold up to 80 people. They were powered by sails and navigated by the stars. The **wa'a** were loaded with food, plants and animals to help them survive the voyage. They also brought seeds and seedlings to plant in their new home.

Name one animal you think they brought and why?

_____

Why would they bring seeds?

_____

Hōkūle'a Wa'a Kaulua

The **Hōkūle'a Wa'a Kaulua (Voyaging Canoe)** shown on the right, built in 1970, is a replica of the original Polynesian canoes. Please read about its creators and follow some of its voyages to other countries on the next page.

As time went on, some of the **wa'a** became smaller and were used for fishing and a way to carry people and goods around the islands. Now they have outrigger **wa'a**, like the picture below, used primarily for sport.

To this day, there is a deep love, respect and connection with the ocean and the Hawaiian people.

Did you know?? Outrigger Canoe Paddling is the official team sport of Hawai'i with over 60 clubs that race. Some paddlers start paddling at the age of 5!

Namolokama Canoe Club

The outrigger wa'a (canoe) has 6 noho (seats). The stroker sits in the front seat and is responsible for setting the pace. The steersperson sits in the back, steers the canoe, and is the captain.

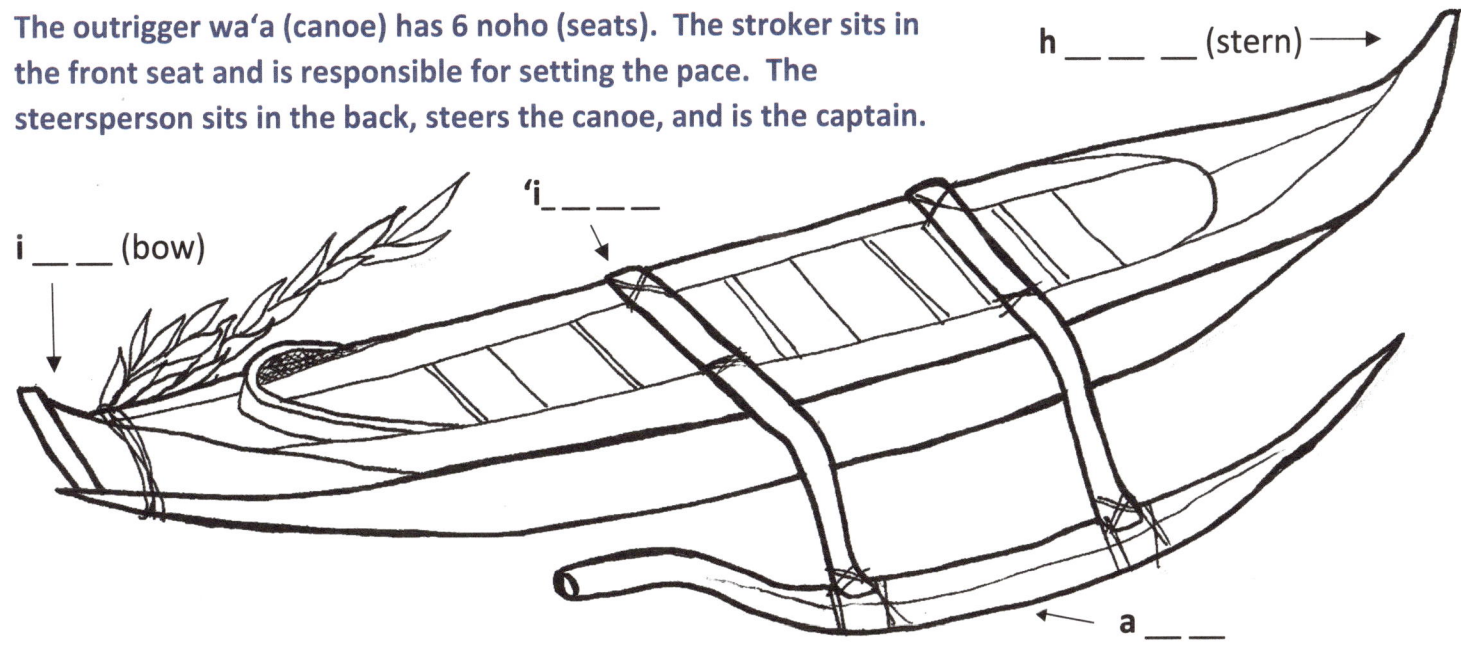

h __ __ __ (stern) ⟶

'i __ __ __ __

i __ __ (bow)

a __ __

Label the parts of the wa'a from the Word Bank -   ama   hope   ihu   'iako

7

The Maze -Start Here

Follow the voyages of the Hōkūleʻa from 2014 to 2017 by navigating through the maze, on its way to Tahiti in 2014 and back home to Hawaii in 2017.

The voyaging vessel "The Hōkūleʻa meaning the "Star of Gladness" is a tribute to the Hawaiian culture past and present. These waʻa became extinct about 600 years ago, until Herb Kane, an artist, envisioned rebuilding them. The Hōkūleʻa is not motorized and has no modern-day electronics to guide her to her destination. She is driven by the sails and the winds of the seas and is guided by the ancient system of navigating by the stars. The original navigator was Mau Piailug from the island of Satawai in Micronesia, who then trained Nainoa Thompson to carry on this great navigating tradition. For the past 41 years she has explored the oceans across the globe. To learn more, go to www.hokulea.com.

The Hawaiian Flag - Read, Learn and Color

The Hawaiian flag is the only flag in America that has been flown to represent a kingdom, a territory, and a state.

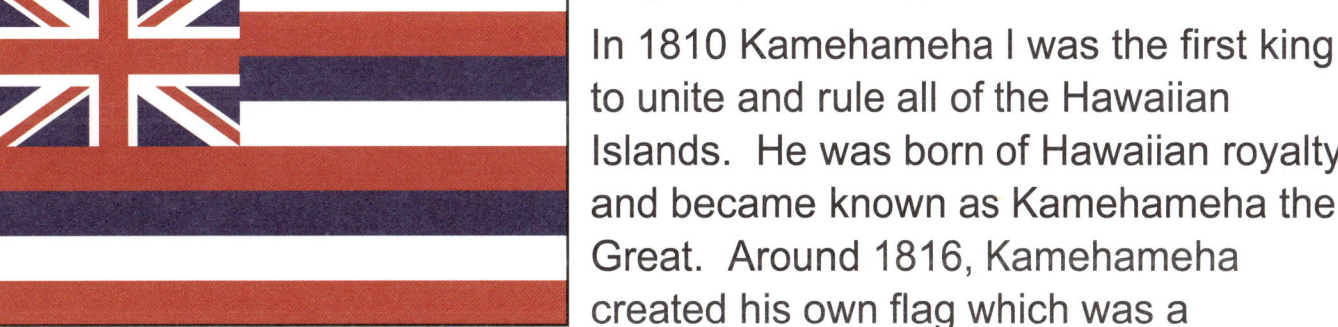

In 1810 Kamehameha I was the first king to unite and rule all of the Hawaiian Islands. He was born of Hawaiian royalty and became known as Kamehameha the Great. Around 1816, Kamehameha created his own flag which was a combination of the British and United States flag to help keep peace and avoid any problems. In about 1845 his flag was altered and was adopted as the Hawaiian State Flag as shown on this page.

The upper-left hand corner of the flag is inspired by the flag of Great Britain and the stripes were inspired by the United States Flag. Each of the eight stripes of red, white and blue represent the islands of Hawai'i as follows: Hawai'i, O'ahu, Kaua'i, Kaho'olawe, Lāna'i, Maui, Moloka'i and Ni'ihau.

9

ALOHA is a Greeting

It is very **nui** (important) how you say **Aloha** (hello or goodbye) to someone. It must be sincere and said with true **Aloha** (love) from the **pu'uwai** (heart). Presenting a **lei** (necklace usually of flowers, leaves or shells) can be a part of this greeting. We can give someone a "**shaka**" (Hawaiian hand gesture to show **Aloha**) with a big **mino'aka** (smile) on your face. In Hawai'i, we also give a **pūliki** (hug) and **honi** (kiss) on the **papālina** (cheek) to say **Aloha** (hello).

All cultures have their own word to say Hello; see if you can match these:

Word for Hello in a different language	Name of the Language or Country
Bonjour	Italian
Konnichiwa	Irish
Ciao	New Zealand/Maori
Dia duit	Japanese
Hujambo	Australia
Hola	Spanish
Namaste	French
Kia ora	Swahili
G' Day	Hindi

Name these 3 countries that speak Spanish: M _ _ _ _ _ _ , S _ _ _ _ , C _ _ _

He aha kou mana'o? (What do you think?) Name another way you can greet or say hello to someone:

10

Hanalei Pier

Hanalei Bay, Kauaʻi
The pier was originally built out of wood before 1892. It was expanded to 340 feet in the early 1900's and a new concrete deck was built. In the 1940's the shed roof was built. Around 1933 the pier became a gathering place for locals, when it was no longer used for shipping rice from Hanalei to Honolulu.

The **shaka**, which means to hang loose, was adopted by Hawaiians as a reminder of a relaxed way of life. A popular way to say hello with your shaka is "Howzit".

Get creative and color your "shaka" below.

How To Make a Lei

Supplies you need to make homemade Hawaiian Leis:
- Colored cardstock or construction paper to cutout flowers
- Dried pasta noodles
- Drinking straws cut into 1 inch pieces
- Paper hole punch
- Colored yarn or thick String
- Floss threader

Directions – Start by cutting your flowers out and use the hole punch to put a hole in the middle of your paper flowers.
Cut the drinking straws into 1" pieces.
Cut your yarn or string into the length for your lei and tie onto the floss threader.   Usually about 40" – 44" in length.
Start threading the flowers, pasta noodles and straws in any pattern you like. (Hint- use different colors of flowers to make your lei brighter.)
When finished tie the ends together and you have your lei!!

Presenting a Lei

Approach the person making eye contact and a **mino'aka** (smile). Put the **lei** over their head onto their shoulders, positioning it with half hanging in the front and half hanging in the back. Then give them a nice **pūliki** (hug) and a **honi** (kiss) on the **papālina** (cheek) passing on your **Aloha** to the person receiving the **lei**.

ALOHA is a Greeting

Pū, pronounced 'poo' is the Hawaiian name for the Conch Shell.

It is considered a **makana** (gift) from the **moana** (ocean) and its sound can travel very long distances.

The blowing of the **Pū** is used for many ceremonies and is a very **nui** (important) part of the Hawaiian culture.

It can have different meanings depending upon how many times it is blown, when it is blown and in which direction it is blown. These meanings are very **kapu** (sacred). Long ago, the blowing of the **Pū** was a way for people to communicate between **nā wa'a** (canoes), across the **moana** and to those on the **'āina** (land). Sometimes it was used to request permission to come to shore.

Permission or denial would then be returned from those on shore by them blowing the **Pū** back with a certain number of blows. Today some people blow the **Pū** to say **Aloha** (goodbye) at sunset to end the day and to say **Mahalo** (thanks).

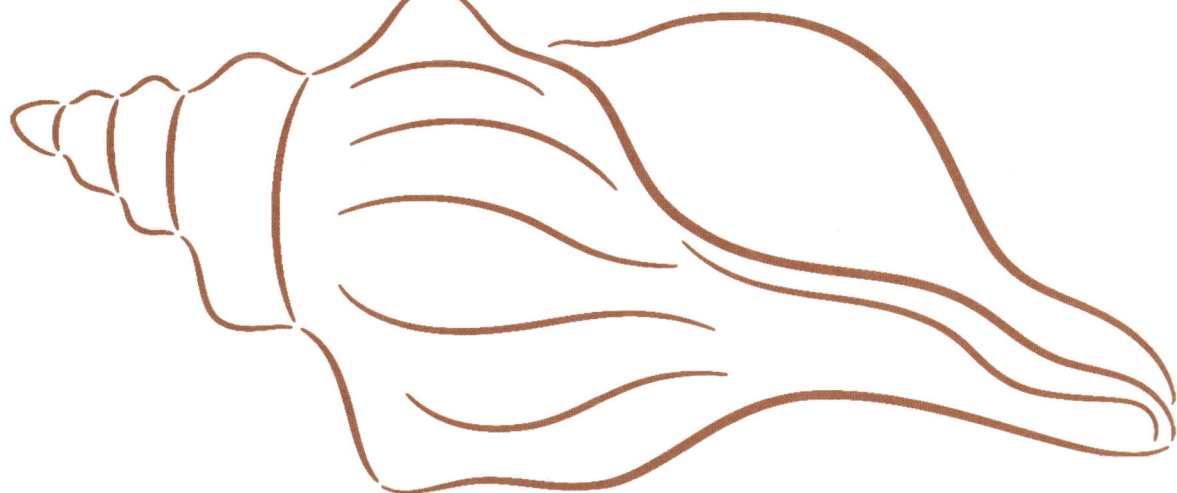

What do you Love?

Color_____

Food_____

Ice Cream_____

Sport_____

Animal_____

Holiday_____

_____

Movie_____

_____

Place_____

_____

'Ohana Time: Tell someone in your 'Ohana why you love them and give them a big pūliki (hug).

ALOHA is Love

American Sign Language for I Love You

Aloha means **unconditional** love in the Hawaiian language. This means we love someone the same; no matter if they are **hau'oli** (happy) or **kaumaha** (sad). Always forgive and have **ahonui** (patience) if they make a mistake. We not only say we **aloha** (love) someone, we also show them through our actions. Such as a **makuahine** (mother) or **makua kāne** (father) hugging their **kamali'i** (children) or a **keiki** (child) hugging their pet to show their **aloha** (love). **He aha kou mana'o?** (What do you think?)

We can never love too many people. In the hearts below list the names of people and ways you can show **aloha** (love).

Names of people you Love

Ways you can show Love

15

ALOHA is PONO

This means living a

ha'aha'a (humble) and decent **ola** (life) by having **maika'i** (good) morals and values. Living a fair and **kūpono** (honest) **ola** (life).

Live your **ola** with peace and fairness, with everyone and in everything you do. Do the right thing and make **maika'i** decisions in your **ola** (life).

A **maika'i** (good) way to practice is to always do what's right, even when no one is looking. Such as when you take a **hele** (walk) on the **kahakai** (beach) and pick up **'ōpala** (trash) instead of leaving it on the ground. **He aha kou mana'o?** (What do you think?)

Listed below are examples of living a PONO LIFE.
Finish the words and write them in the star.

#1. -You have a test at school and someone gives you the answers to the test. It would be easy to use the answers, but you know it's not right and decide to do it on your own. By doing this you are being **h__n__s t.**

#2. – You get really mad at your friend for breaking your favorite skateboard. You find out later that it was an accident and feel bad about getting so upset, so you go to your friend and apologize for getting so mad.
It takes **c__u__a__e** to apologize.

#3. – Your Dad asks you to mow the lawn, when your friends come by and ask you to go play a game of soccer. You are really tempted to go play and mow the lawn later, but decide to stay and do as your Dad asked.
By doing this you are being **r__s__o__s__bl__.**

Listed below are a few words that describe ways to live Pono. See if you can unscramble these words and practice them in your life:

ienc _ _ _ _   **cpetrse** _ _ _ _ _ _ _   **velo** _ _ _ _   **tsurt** _ _ _ _ _   **gvnigi** _ _ _ _ _ _

'Ohana Time – Decide with your 'ohana a place you would like to cleanup and pick up the trash.

BE PONO

ALAKA'I: *The value of leadership. Lead with initiative, and with your good example. You shall be the guide for others when you have gained their trust and respect.*

17

ALOHA is Kindness

This means showing compassion, caring and generosity from the **pu'uwai** (heart). Treat everyone with kindness and be an **'olu'olu** (nice) person. You can show kindness through your **'ōlelo** (words) and your actions. Make someone **mino'aka** (smile) by giving them a real, sincere compliment. Being **'olu'olu** to others, not only makes them feel **maika'i** (good), but it makes you feel **maika'i** too!

When you go out to **he'e nalu** (surf) with your **hoaloha** (friend), cheer him on and let him get the **set wave** (best wave).

He aha kou mana'o? (What do you think?)

Make and take the **olu'olu'** pledge and share it with everyone.

Every day, I promise to be olu'olu' **to everyone by greeting them with a smile and** _____.

Fill in the sentences with 3 different ways you can be kind to your friends.

#1. I help my friends_____.

#2. I tell my friends_____.

#3. I share _____**with my friends.**

Aloha Kindness Package: The next time someone does something nice, thank them by making a kindness package. In the back of the book on page 47, you will find 2 wrappers you can cut out and use or make your own. Take the wrapper and put a piece of candy or small gift, then wrap it up, tie the ends with a 10" raffia or ribbon and tape the back closed.

'Ohana Time - Do something that is really kind for one of your 'ohana and then ask them to do something really kind for someone else and keep passing on kind deeds.

Aloha Surf Sponsor

The Aloha Surf Sponsor is designing a quiver (surfboard collection) of Kindness Surfboards that are given to the kindest guys and girls on the surf tour.

The first board is the **'olu'olu** (nice) surfboard already designed and ready to go.

They need your help to design the remaining three. The names of the boards, shown below in blue, stand for what a nice person is all about.

#1. The first board will be labeled **Pu'uwai** (heart), because all kind guys and girls have great hearts.

#2. The second board will be labeled **Hoaloha** (friend), because kind guys and girls are good friends.

#3. The third board will be labeled **Pono** (integrity), because kind guys and girls do the right thing.

Now label each board with one of the words above, then design and color the quiver of surfboards.

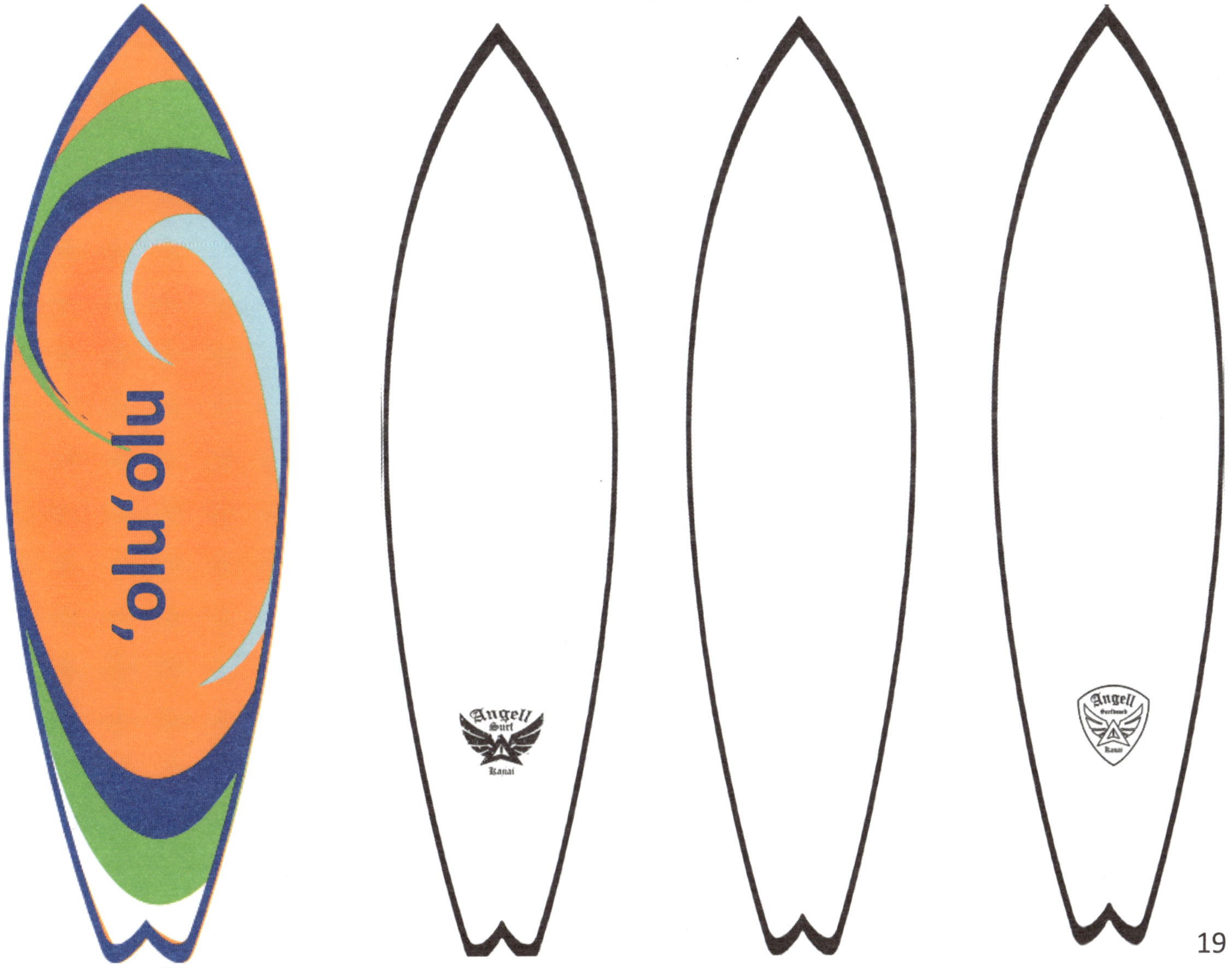

'olu'olu

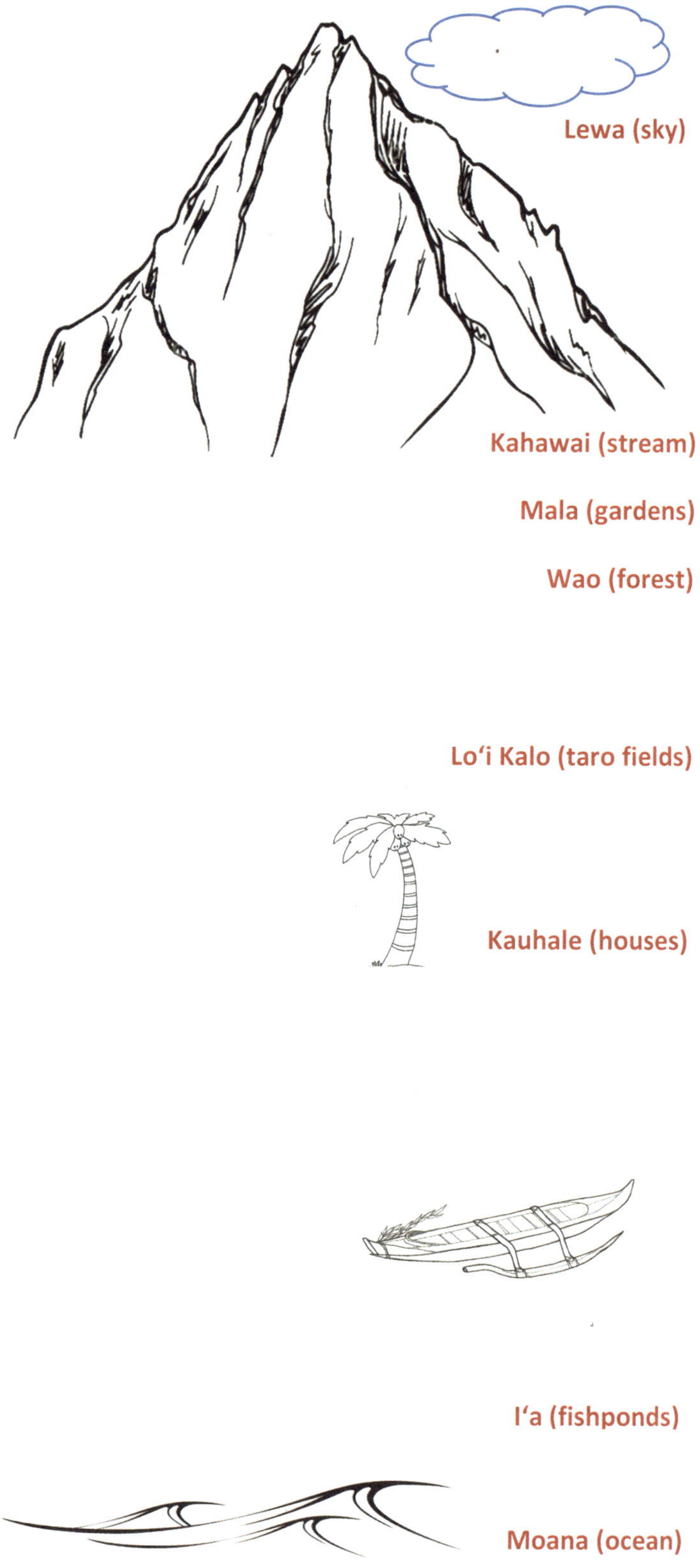

Lewa (sky)

Kahawai (stream)

Mala (gardens)

Wao (forest)

Lo'i Kalo (taro fields)

Kauhale (houses)

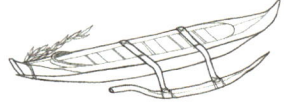

I'a (fishponds)

Moana (ocean)

As Hawaiian people we have a kuleana to our 'āina (land). We care for it and respect it, and then in return, our 'āina has the kuleana to feed, shelter, and clothes us. By keeping this balance, we will always be taken care of.   **Illustration by Matt Foster.**

An ahupua'a, is a pie-shaped land division ▲ *that starts mauka (top of the mountain) to makai (to the ocean). As you can see by the picture the 'āina was divided up into sections starting at the top with the lewa, mala, wao, kula, kauhale, lo'i kalo, loko i'a to the moana. It is very important to know that a kahawai (stream) started at the top of the mountain and ran down the middle of the ahupua'a to the moana. This provided the water needed for crops, drinking and to sustain life. All the people living in the ahupua'a had a job to do like taking care of plants and animals, harvesting, building to provide for each other. Everyone was taken care of in the ahupua'a* ***Now draw and color in all of the sections of the***

20   ***ahupua'a above on the right, by using the picture on the left as your guide. Get creative!***

ALOHA is Kuleana

This means responsibility.
Everyone has their own **kuleana** (responsibility) with themselves, others and the **honua** (world) around them. We accept our **kuleana** with commitment and privilege, no matter if it's something we are excited about doing or something that feels more like a chore. Your **kuleana** can be as simple as cleaning your room or as **nui** (important) as protecting the **ʻāina** (land), saving endangered animals or becoming a navigator on Hōkūleʻa. **He aha kou manaʻo?** (What do you think?)

Ulu- (Breadfruit) Tree

Circle the chores below that are your kuleana.

Mow the lawn

Fold the laundry

Clean your room

Wash the dishes

Babysit your brother or sister

Do your homework

Take out the trash

Clean the garage

Feed the Dog

Yardwork

Help Cook

Wash the car/truck

Color the picture above: My **kuleana** as **haumana** (student) is to learn by listening, understanding and practicing what the **kumu** (teacher) will **aʻo** (teach) me about **Aloha**, culture and tradition and why it is **nui**. What is the **kuleana** of the **kumu**?

ALOHA is Mana

Mana is a powerful energy energy that can be positive or negative. Aloha is filled with <u>positive</u> **mana**. It can come from a **wahi** (place), **kanaka** (person), **mea** (thing) or idea. Your Aloha is stronger by welcoming positive **mana**. When positive **mana** fills your **puʻuwai** (heart) it makes you feel **maikaʻi** (good) and warm inside. Like **ka lā** (the sun) shining down and warming you up on a beautiful sandy **kahakai** (beach) in **Hawaiʻi**.
He aha kou manaʻo? (What do you think?)

Write one word that *tells how you feel* when you see:

-A Honu   - A Heart   -A Smiley Face
                   Puʻuwai

_____   _____   _____

Maunakea is a very special place to the Hawaiian people and all people. It is a spiritual and *wahi kapu* (sacred place) that has powerful **mana**. It is culturally, environmentally and historically significant. We must show respect.

Share your Positive Mana - fill in the blanks: I will fill my puʻuwai 💙 with p_____e

mana. I will always try to see the _____ in everyone and always offer to

_____ when someone is in need. I will greet others with a big 🙂 s_____

and encouraging w_____.   Be the best you can be – "BE MANAFUL".

Directions:

1. Aloha is filled with positive Mana. Like a warm feeling from a special place that makes you feel maika'i (good) inside, such as the picture on the left with the beautiful sunset, ocean and surfer.

2. Do you like the color? _____

3. Does the picture make you feel good? _____

4. Name a place that makes you feel maika'i? _____

5. Now color the picture below with crayons or colored pencils, using all your favorite colors.

Think about those colors and things that make you feel good inside.

'Ohana Time- Where does your 'ohana like to spend time?

Mālama the __ __ __ __ (Hawaiian word for turtle)

You can have a career that helps malama our oceans by becoming a Microbiologist or Marine Biologist.

Use Word Box to fill in the blanks below :   microbes   living   eye   whales   bacteria   plankton   ocean

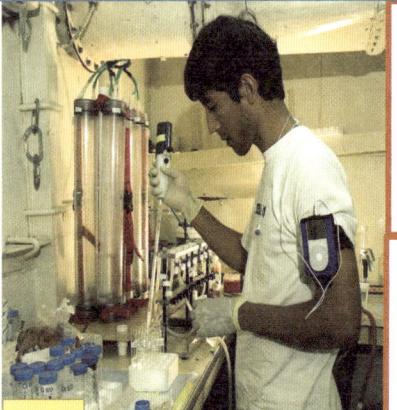

#1

Marine Biology is the study of l _ _ _ _ _ things in the o _ _ _ _. They study the tiniest p _ _ _ _ _ _ _ to the largest w _ _ _ _ _.
Which picture is the Marine Biologist checking the coral reef? Write in the #_____

Microbiologists study b _ _ _ _ _ _ _, m_ _ _ _ _ _ and other viruses that are invisible to the human _ _ _.   Which picture is the Microbiologist doing biological testing on seawater samples? Write in the #___

#2

ALOHA is Mālama

This means to care for all

things; like the **ʻāina** (land), your **ʻohana** (family), your **nā hoaloha** (friends), yourself and all living creatures. Such as, helping free a **honu** (turtle) that is tangled up in plastic, from **ʻōpala** (garbage) in the **moana** (ocean). Make sure when you're in the **moana,** not to stand on the **ʻāpapa** (reef). It can kill the **koʻa** (corals) which are made up of many living organisms and home to many **iʻa** (fish).

What else can we do to protect the reef? (Hint) (Fill in the blanks)

R _ _ _ _   F _ _ _ _ _ _ _ _

S _ _ _ _ _ _ _ _ _

Unscramble below things you do to take care of:

Yourself	ʻĀina (land)
#1. **R X E C S E I**	#1. **Y E R L C E C**
_ _ _ _ _ _ _ _ _	_ _ _ _ _ _ _
#2. **A E T L H A T E H Y**	#2. **C P K I P U S A T H R**
_ _ _	_ _ _ _ _ _
_ _ _ _ _ _ _	_ _ _ _ _

Help Take Care of Our WORLD

He aha kou manaʻo? (What do you think?)
Write how you **mālama** the two things shown below.

#3. Yourself _____   #3. ʻĀina _____

> ***Did you know??*** Hundreds of thousands of honu, whales, and other marine life, and more than 1 million seabirds die each year from ocean pollution and ingestion or entanglement in marine debris. Marine debris is garbage thrown into the ocean. Learn more at http://www.seeturtles.org/ocean-plastic & https://www.surfrider.org/

Top Ten Marine Litter Items

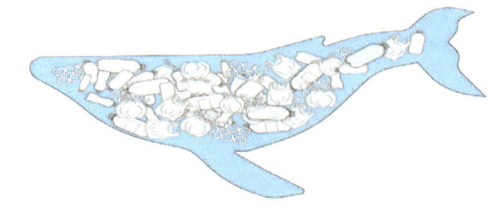

Marine litter is garbage/trash such as glass and plastic that pollutes our oceans. About 70 percent of this litter sinks to the floor of the ocean and some remains floating in the water, harming our sea life. We must Mālama the ocean.

Listed below are the top ten things that litter our oceans and the amount found. See if you can match the number on the left (#1 is the highest) with the trash items on the right, found in our oceans today. Draw a line between the number and the picture.

#1. 25,000,000 pieces

#2. 9,700,000 pieces

#3. 9,400,000 pieces

#4. 9,200,000 pieces

#5. 7,400,000 pieces

#6. 5,700,000 pieces

#7. 4,900,000 pieces

#8. 4,800,000 pieces

#9. 4,500,000 pieces

#10. 2,200,000 pieces

Disposable plates/cups/forks/knives and spoons

Glass Bottles

Rope

Cigarettes

Food containers/wrappers

Plastic Bottles

Bags – Paper and Plastic

Straws

Beverage Cans

Lids and Caps

Underwater World of Hawai'i

Meet the Humpback Whale, Green Sea Turtle, Monk Seal and the Spotted Jellyfish.   Color them and answer the questions below.

#1. We are all mammals.   True or False

#2. We all have gills.   True or False

#3. We all live and swim in the moana. True or False

#4. We are all endangered species.   True or False

#5. We all live in the coral reef.   True or False

#6. We are all carnivores.   True or False

#7. The ocean covers 71% of the earth. True or False

27

ALOHA is Respect

This means showing consideration to people, places, animals, things, ideas and yourself. When you show **hō'ihi** (respect), you act in a way that shows you care. In **Hawai'i** we greet **kūpuna** (elders) as **'Anakē** (Aunty/Auntie) or **'Anakala** (Uncle). When entering a **hale** (house) always leave your **kalipa** (slippers/flip flops) outside the door. When visiting a **heiau** (sacred site) be careful of where you **holo** (walk) and do not take or damage anything. To receive respect, you must give respect. **He aha kou mana'o?** (What do you think?)

Read each sentence and circle the word that applies -Respectful or Disrespectful:

Gossiping behind someone's back. **Respectful** or **Disrespectful**

Holding the door open for a **kupuna**? **Respectful** or **Disrespectful**

Interrupting someone when they are speaking. **Respectful** or **Disrespectful**

Texting on your phone at the dinner table. **Respectful** or **Disrespectful**

Showing up an hour late to meet with your swim coach. **Respectful** or **Disrespectful**

Can you please help me download this app? **Respectful** or **Disrespectful**

Using your manners is a way to show respect: Draw a line between the following questions with the correct response shown in English and Hawaiian.

#1. When you receive a gift you say?   EXCUSE ME - E KALA MAI

#2. What do you say if you bump into someone?   THANK YOU - MAHALO

#3. When you ask for help you say?   SORRY - KAUMAHA

#4. If you hurt someone's feelings, you say?   PLEASE - 'OLU'OLU

28

DESIGN YOUR HALE (House)
How do you want it to look?

#1. What color is the **sand** on your beach or the color of the **wai** (water)?

#2. What color will the **thatched roof** and walls be?

#3. Will it have **pua** (flowers)?

#4. What **color** are your **kalipa** outside the front door?

#5. Do you have a **cat**, dog or maybe a **pig**?

#6. Do you have **surfboards** or a bike outside?

Get Creative with your hale!

'Ohana Time- Talk about someone you respect and why.

29

Ānuenue (rainbow)

The colors of the ānuenue are red, orange, yellow, green, blue, indigo (blue/purple) and purple. We cannot touch it, because it is like a see-through picture made by sun and water. Sunlight is made up of all the colors in the ānuenue, but our eyes can only see it when the sun's rays shine through rain. The sun's rays actually bend and lets us see the colors!
****

The Good and Bad Choice Jars

Using the words list, write the word on the labels that apply to the jars shown below.

Cheating	Healthy Lifestyle
Honesty	Smoking
Stealing	Bullying
Addiction	Kindness
Giving	Gossiping
Truthful	Hard Work
Lying	Commitment

Good Choices

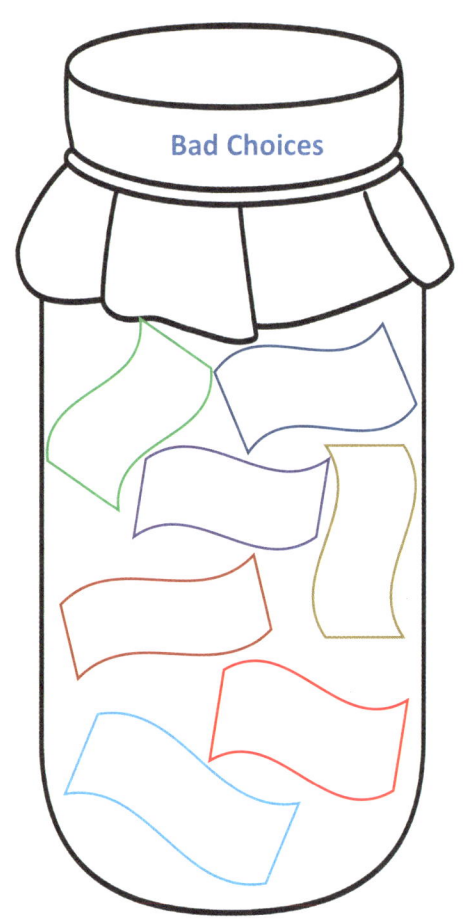

Bad Choices

ALOHA is Light

Pu'uwai   **Pu'uwai**

This means living a **ola** (life) of goodness. Always choose the path of **maika'i** (good) over bad. Live, **'ōlelo** (talk) and act from a **pu'uwai** (heart) full of **Aloha**. Sometimes, standing up for the right thing is not easy. It takes a lot of **ikaika** (strength) and **koa** (courage) to make the right choice and follow the path of light.

Such as standing up for someone that is being made fun of and teased. It takes **ikaika** and **koa** to stand up for others and when you do, it makes you feel **maika'i** inside, like the radiant colors of the **ānuenue** (rainbow). **He aha kou mana'o?** (What do you think?)

> If someone was being made fun of, what would you do?
> A. Walk Away B. Pretend you didn't see. C. Help in any way you can.

Color your ānuenue (rainbow) below with any colors you want that represent your koa (courage) and ikaika (strength). Let your light and ānuenue shine bright!

Ikaika   Koa

Fun Facts about Hawai'i

Across

2 Small fish under 10 pounds (pg.43)

5 House in Hawaiian (pg.29)

6 Endangered Seal (pg.27)

7 Hawaiian word for Thank You (pg.28)

9 Hawaiian hand gesture to show Aloha (pg.10)

10 _____canoe (pg.7)

12 The Hawaiian Islands are in what ocean (pg.4)

14 Hawaiian name for slippers or flip flops (pg.28)

15 The color purple in Hawaiian (pg.4)

16 A necklace of flowers or shells (pg.10)

Down

1 Leaves from this tree are used for weaving (pg.35)

3 Family in Hawaiian (pg.25)

4 Turtle in Hawaiian (pg.25)

6 Ocean in Hawaiian (pg.25)

8 Tallest mountain in the world (pg.5)

9 An ocean sport (pg.46)

11 A mountain that erupts and emits lava (pg.5)

13 Child in Hawaiian (pg.15)

15 Thick paste to eat made from kalo or taro (pg.3)

16 Hawaiian Feast (pg.3)

Hawaiian Wordsearch
ʻŌlelo Hawaiʻi

S	U	E	I	K	K	A	Ē	K	E	A	A	A	A	K	A	M	M	A	L
A	N	U	P	U	K	A	H	A	K	A	I	A	ʻ	H	I	H	L	Ī	E
P	O	E	O	A	U	Ō	I	A	S	A	ʻ	Ā	O	H	E	Ō	A	U	U
A	H	A	N	A	A	K	K	A	K	H	I	L	H	N	K	A	I	U	A
P	Ō	L	O	K	A	I	U	U	A	N	A	M	A	N	Ō	K	M	E	U
Ō	W	O	K	N	U	O	E	L	A	H	W	K	N	L	I	P	P	Ā	N
N	L	A	Ē	N	H	M	Ā	L	A	M	A	N	A	E	L	U	K	L	K
H	U	K	L	U	I	H	U	M	A	L	H	Ō	K	Ū	L	E	ʻ	A	Ī
I	H	A	L	U	ʻ	H	Ē	L	K	H	N	Ū	U	E	A	Ō	A	H	H
P	I	A	O	P	A	H	I	A	L	A	K	ʻ	A	A	N	K	U	O	K

WORD LIST:

ʻĀINA	HULA	KUMU	ʻOHANA
AKUA	KAHAKAI	KUPUNA	PONO
ALOHA	KAI	LEI	PULE
HALE	KEIKI	MAHALO	SHAKA
HAWAIʻI	KŌKUA	MĀLAMA	
HŌKŪLEʻA	KULA	MANA	
HONU	KULEANA	MANŌ	

33

ALOHA is Kōkua

This means giving of yourself

to **kōkua** (help) when needed and make the **honua** (world) a better place. It is important to **kōkua** without expecting something in return, except maybe a simple **mahalo** (thank you). It is important to say **mahalo**, if someone offers to **kōkua** you. Also, if you need **kōkua,** never be afraid to ask.

As **kamaliʻi** (children), we can **kōkua** deliver **mea ʻai** (food) in the "**Aloha Truck**", to **kūpuna** (elders) in the **kaiaulu** (community), so they are healthy and **ikaika** (strong). **He aha kou manaʻo?** (What do you think?)

Make a list of things you can do at your house and in your community to help others:

Hale (House) List

Kaiaulu (Community) List

1._____

2._____

3._____

1._____

2._____

3._____

Write a story about how you would **kokua** someone, using the **Hawaiian** words in the Word Bank:

Word Bank: **kōkua**   **hoaloha** (friend)   **mahalo**   **ʻekolu** (three)   **ʻulaʻula** (red)

_____

_____

_____

_____

_____

_____

ʻOhana Time: Write down a way you and your ʻohana can kōkua to make the honua a better place!

Color and Label the HALA TREE

Scientific Name - Pandanus tectorius

Parts of the Hala Tree – Label with the highlighted name listed below.

#1. Aerial Roots (ule hala) also known as "Prop Roots"

#2. Lau Hala (leaves)

#3. Trunk

#4. Fruit

#5. Keys (each fruit can contain up to 50 keys) When dried they were used as a brush to paint on kapa cloth.

#6. Canopy (can be up to 40 feet across)

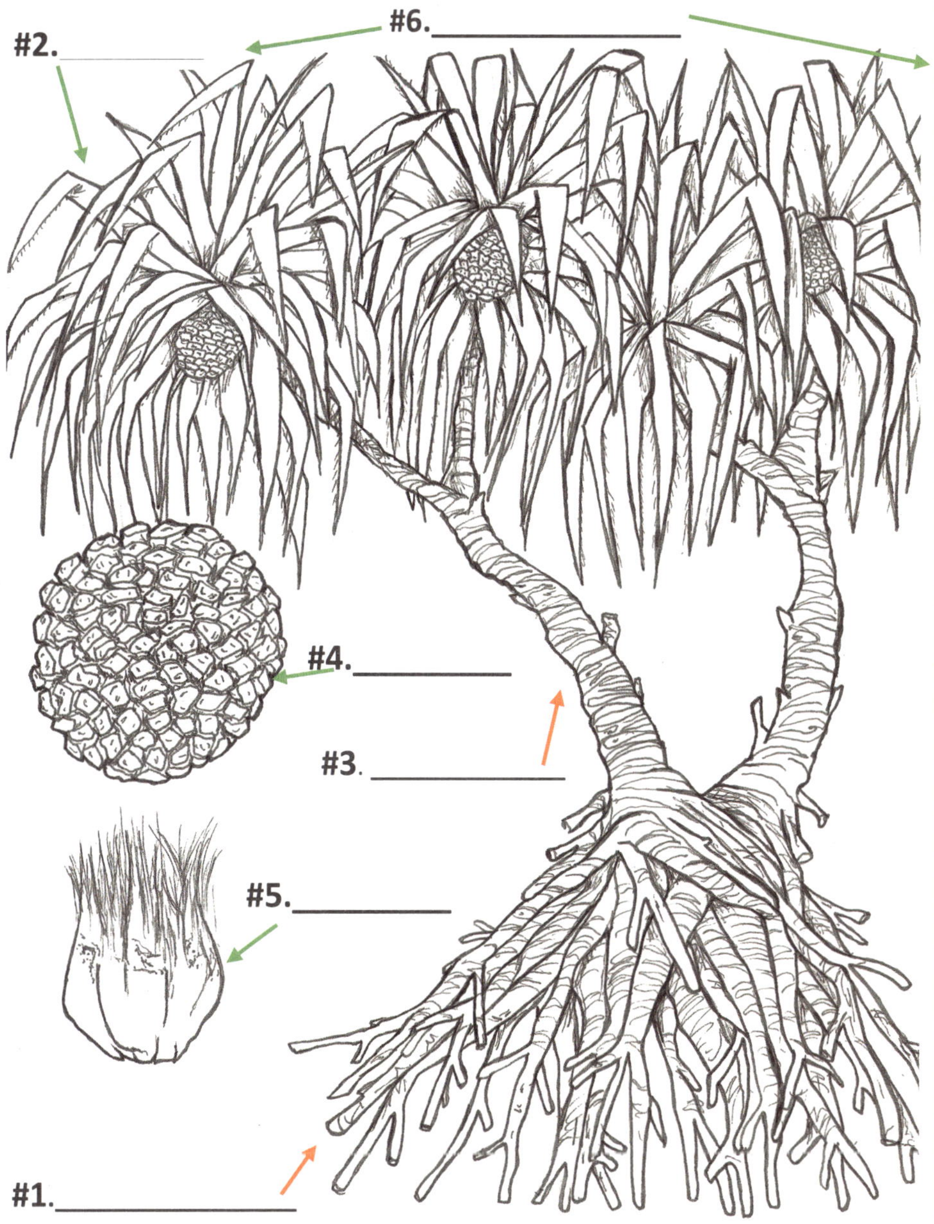

#2._____

#6._____

#4._____

#3._____

#5._____

#1._____

Not only do we give of ourselves to **kōkua**, but so does the **honua** (world) around us. A perfect example is the Hala, which is a native tree of Hawai'i.

The leaves of the Hala are called **lau** (meaning leaf) hala, which are long and twisted with sharp edges. When dried and stripped they are woven by weavers into many items such as mats, bracelets, hats, bags and fan. They were also used for thatching roofs.

The female tree bears a fruit that looks similar to a pineapple. When the fruit falls on the ground it breaks up into little pieces called keys. When they dry they can be used like paint brushes.

The first Polynesians also brought Hala, which they used to weave the sails for their canoes.

35

ALOHA IS HOPE

#1. Think of a powerful message that could make a positive change in the world.

#2. An example would be:

Always kōkua each other

Do you remember what kōkua means?

#3. Write your message here first and then draw it on the wall below.

_____

_____

#4. **Now color your message on the wall below.**

Did you know? Local and international artists gather for a week-long festival and let their imagination run free with their "Street Art" in the district of Kakaʻako on Oahu. Drawing on public structures is illegal without permission.

HOʻOMAU:
The value of perseverance. To persist, to continue, to perpetuate. Never give up.

ALOHA is Hope

Mana'olana (hope) is to never give up on anything you mana'o'i'o (believe) in or are trying to achieve. Stay positive, hana (work) hard and believe that anything is possible. Always seek and strive to see the maika'i (good) in all things. Such as a honua (world) of acceptance without discrimination or a honua with maluhia (peace) without war. Imagine a honua full of Aloha.

He aha kou mana'o?
(What do you think)?

Name one thing you would never give up on:_____

If you think it, you can make it happen!

A Honua Full of:

Unscramble the words in the world that ⟶ give us hope.

Sdnkeins _ _ _ _ _ _ _ _

veol _ _ _ _

Asifnres _ _ _ _ _ _ _ _

nysohet _ _ _ _ _ _ _

ethlah _ _ _ _ _ _

pieshpans _ _ _ _ _ _ _ _ _

Yjo _ _ _

turgtdeai _ _ _ _ _ _ _ _ _

ecpae _ _ _ _ _

Dream BIG and Never Lose Hope

'Ohana Time- Discuss with your 'ohana and decide together on something you would like to improve. We can improve on_____

SUPPORT DIVERSITY

**If you see something wrong,
stand up and (be strong),
be IKAIKA**

FA**I**R

_____

K

_____

A

_____

I

_____

K

_____

A

_____

Using the word Ikaika above. Write words that support diversity and do not discriminate. The first one has been done for you. by using the first letter I – we wrote the word FAIR. Possible words are Accept, Teamwork, Unity, Race, Nationality and Friends. Just ideas.

ALOHA is Openness

This means to accept po'e (people) or things as they are and not be judgmental. Don't judge **kahi** (someone) for what they **ha'i** (say) or do, without getting to know them. Make sure you know all the **nū hou** (information), before you make a decision about **kahi** or something. Treat others as you want to be treated. Such as being **'olu'olu** (nice) to a new kid in **kula** (school) or the new **keiki** (kid) on the block even if they **kūlike** (look), **'olelo** (talk) or dress differently than you. Show them they are appreciated and that they belong. **Aloha** does not fear or discriminate.

He aha kou mana'o? (What do you think?)

Have you ever been the new kid in school, in a sport, in a group of friends or in the neighborhood? If so which one? _____

How did it feel to be the new kid? _____
_____

It's great to be me. - Draw a picture of yourself here.

I have _____ colored hair.

My hair is short or long. (circle one)

I have _____ colored eyes.

My skin is _____ color.

I do or do not have freckles. (circle one)

I do or do not wear glasses. (circle one)

My ancestors come from _____.
                    (name of state, nation and/or countries)

I love to _____.

Aloha is Openness

Friends
Forever
Pōhai
Celeste
Rae

DRAW YOUR MESSAGE IN THE SAND

"Manini"- Convict Tang

Ahi – Yellowfin Tuna

We are all fish but we sure look different, just like people!

Mahimahi

"Uhu" - Parrotfish

Did you know?? There are over 1,100 fish species in the Hawaiian Islands of which 149 are endemic (native to Hawai'i).

SURFING SAFARI

```
                    G
                  C O O
                A A O R K
              R B A F E M C
              V F W K Y V I E A
            E Z I O X F I K R P B
          N J P O Z G O U W A X Z T
        L O K K N N P O Q I T K T W U
      Z E S V U I N I T B A R R E L E C
    F C A E I P H W I B J G W I P E O U T
  N S M S R P X A F V G N Q V E E L D D A P
    Q X H I G V N S R D U C K D I V E H Q
      C R D E I P O A E R I A L H C T H
        R E N L M Q U P C E V R Z U D
          E D R A O B F R U S K O E
            T O Y U Y T J R H E K
              A A G G R O J S O
                O X N O E O T
                  L Z E L S
                    F C Y
                      G
```

WORD LIST:

SURFBOARD	KOOK	NOSERIDE	CARVE
STOKED	BARREL	DUCKDIVE	FLOATER
GROM	WIPEOUT	CLOSEOUT	AGGRO
WAVE	PADDLE	CUTBACK	LEASH
RIPPING	QUIVER	GOOFYFOOT	AERIAL

ALOHA

ALOHA is Sharing

This means living a **manawaleʻa** (generous) **ola** (life), unselfishly and without **ʻālunu** (greed). If you have more than you need or more than you want, then **mahele** (share) willingly with others that might not be so fortunate. You can **mahele** your time, belongings and **manaʻo** (ideas). **Mahele** (share) **Aloha** every day. **He aha kou manaʻo?** (What do you think?) A way to share is to give, by helping great causes through charities called non-profits.

What's your great idea?

You are going to start your own charity/non-profit corporation. But before you start, read below about some real-life examples of non-profits started by kids to help inspire you. As you're reading think about how you can help in the world and come up with your own ideas.

#1. HANNAH TAYLOR started THE LADYBUG FOUNDATION at just 8 years old. She saw a homeless man eating out of a garbage can and wanted to help. The charity helps keep homeless people safe, with a place to live and food. She has raised over $2 million dollars. Check it out www.ladybugfoundation.org.

#2. ALEX SCOTT started ALEX'S LEMONADE FOUNDATION at 4 years old. She was diagnosed with cancer and decided to raise money to help other kids with cancer. With her first lemonade stand she raised $2,000.00. Alex passed away at 8 and had raised over $1million dollars. Check it out www.alexslemonade.org.

#3. AUSTIN GUTWEIN started HOOPS OF HOPE at 9 years old when he watched a video about kids that had lost their parents to AIDS and decided he wanted to help the kids. Through his hoop-a-thon they've raised over $3million. **Austin wants to tell people to do something and don't sit on the side lines. Just start where you are with anything and you can change the world.

Now it's your turn. On pages 44 and 45, answer the questions, color and design your poster for the world! Help start and support your great cause!!

WE NEED YOUR HELP!

42

Yellowfin Tuna is known as **'Ahi** in Hawai'i. The **'Ahi** is one of the larger tuna species and can weigh up to 400 pounds (400 lbs.)

Question? If you catch a 375 lb. **'Ahi** and give each family 15 pounds of fish to eat, how many families could you feed? _____

Aloha is Sharing: Like when you go **lawai'a** (fishing), feed your **'ohana** (family), then share the rest of the **i'a** (fish) you catch with your **hoaloha** (friend). **COLOR YOUR FISH!**

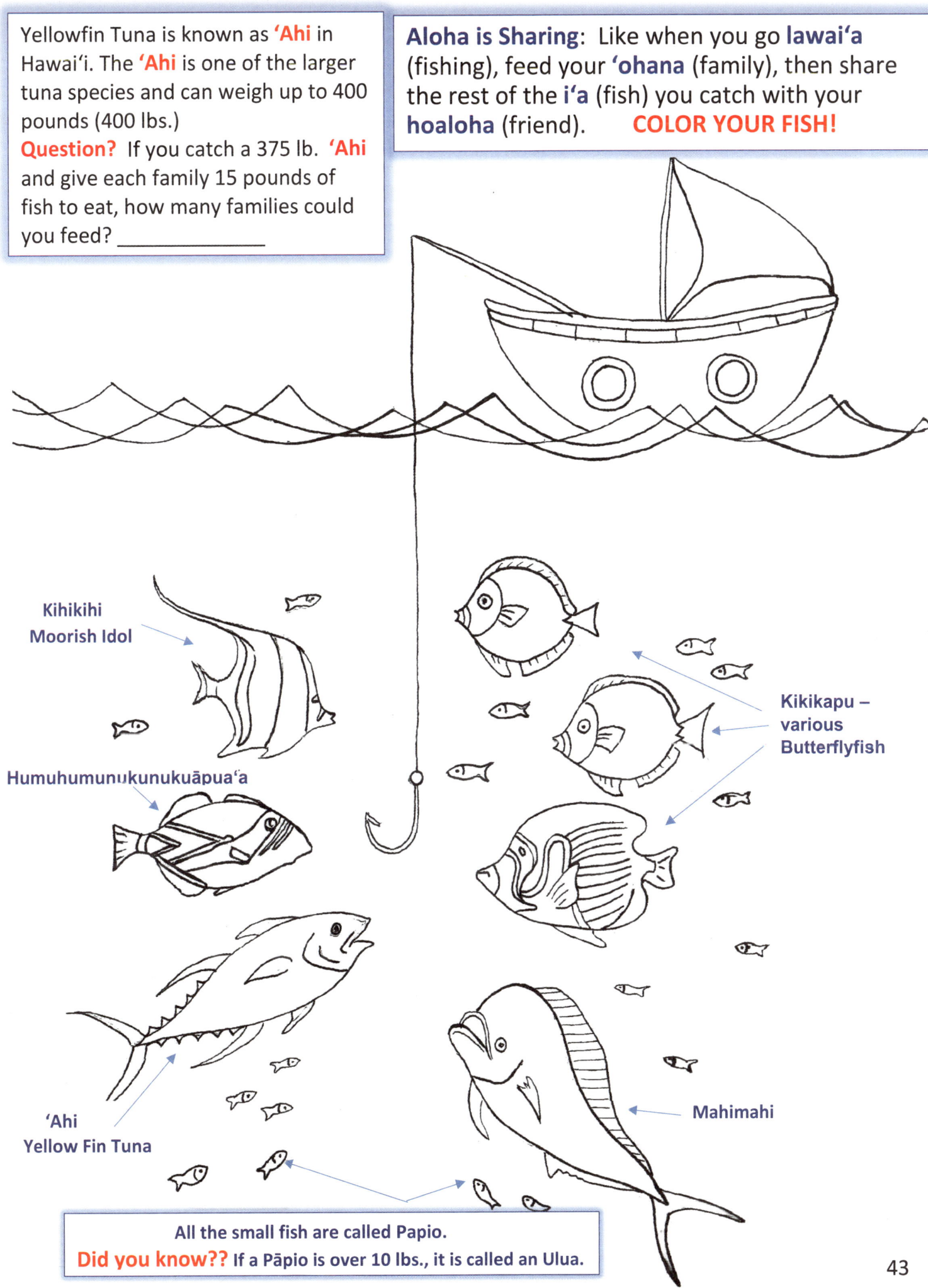

Kihikihi
Moorish Idol

Humuhumunukunukuāpua'a

Kikikapu –
various
Butterflyfish

'Ahi
Yellow Fin Tuna

Mahimahi

All the small fish are called Papio.

Did you know?? If a Pāpio is over 10 lbs., it is called an Ulua.

CREATE A CAUSE   **Now it's your turn. We will use the bubble diagram below to brainstorm ideas for your non-profit.** As you answer the questions 1-4, place your answers in the corresponding bubbles that are marked 1-4.   When you have your bubble diagram complete, you will be ready to design your poster.   Remember to re-read the examples to get ideas.

#1. What is your cause? Who or what do you want to **kōkua** (help)? (use bubbles marked #1)

#2. Once you know where and what you want to help, you are ready to name your non-profit. Remember it can be anything you want.

#3. How will you raise money? You can make and sell something or ask for donations.

#4. Once you get the money, what will you do with it to help your cause?

#5. How much money do you want to raise? You will need to figure out how much you need to help your cause. Example - $1,000 could feed 100 homeless people.

Congratulations, you have finished your bubble diagram and are now ready to create your poster to raise money for your cause/charity.

#1. Take the information from bubbles #1 and take that information to put under **"We Kōkua"** (help) on the poster, to let people know what your cause is and who or what you want to help.

#2. Take the information in bubble #2 and write it above **"A Non-Profit Corporation"**.

#3. Take the information from bubbles # 3 and put it under **"You Can"** (telling people how to raise money).

#4. Take the information from bubbles #4 and put under **"We Need"** to let people know what you will do with the money.

#5. Take the information in bubble #5 and put under **"Our Goal is to Raise $_____"**.

#6. Now you can color and decorate your poster anyway you like. Add more pictures, words or designs.   **Congratulations – you can now Share by giving.**

A Non-Profit Corporation

We Kōkua

We need

You can

Our Goal is to Raise $ _____

Practice your Hawaiian. Match the pictures with the Hawaiian name by drawing a line to the English word on the right.

lawaiʻa

hale

lau

puʻuwai

minoʻaka

heʻe nalu

moana

honua

ānuenue

ʻohana

la

kalo

waʻa

nā maka

ʻōpala

kula

honu

taro

family

trash or garbage

eyes

house

heart

surfing

turtle

ocean

fishing

leaf

school

rainbow

smile

sun

world

canoe

ALOHA

"Mahalo or Thank You"
For Being Such a Nice Person!

Kindness Wrappers - Cut out on the dotted lines and follow instructions on Aloha is Kindness page.

ALOHA

"Mahalo or Thank You"
For Being Such a Nice Person!

MAHALO
"Thank you", as a way of living.
Live in thankfulness for the richness that
makes life so precious.

From:_____

MAHALO
"Thank you", as a way of living.
Live in thankfulness for the richness that
makes life so precious.

From:_____